CW00548071

A TRIBUTE TO
The Modest Member
BERT KELLY

Occasional Papers 60

A TRIBUTE TO
The Modest Member
BERT KELLY

THE CENTRE FOR
INDEPENDENT
STUDIES

1997

Published June 1997 by

The Centre for Independent Studies Limited.

Views expressed in the publications of The Centre for Independent
Studies are those of the authors and do not necessarily reflect the views
of the Centre's staff, Advisers, Directors or officers.

National Library of Australia

Cataloguing–in–Publication Data:

ISBN 1 86432 022 2.

1. Kelly, C.R. (Charles Robert), 1912-1997. 2. Kelly,C.R.
(Charles Robert), 1912-1997 - Views on economics. 3.
Politicians - Australia - Biography. 4. Legislators -
Australia - Biography. 5. Cabinet officers - Australia -
Biography. I. Centre for Independent Studies (Aus-
tralia). (Series : CIS occasional papers ; 60).

328.94092

Contents

Foreword

When Bert Kelly died on January 17, 1997 at the age of 84, the life of a remarkable and dedicated man was over. But the mission to which he devoted much of his long life was still alive in the minds of Bert's friends and supporters. Bert is remembered primarily for his commitment to the cause of free trade and economic good sense, but also for his ability to communicate his ideas clearly, incisively and, as was his style, with humour. It is a tribute to him that he has been widely acknowledged as having been a pioneer in this debate in Australia, a debate which by and large has been won. Part of his legacy is that Australia is now a far more open and competitive society and economy than has been the case for much of this century.

As a tribute to Bert Kelly, the Centre for Independent Studies arranged a function in Melbourne in March 1997 where a number of individuals, all friends and admirers of Bert, could say a few words so that we all might get a clearer measure of this great Australian. We designated this as the first of the 1997 Bert Kelly series of lectures and seminars.

Politics clearly paid a big role in Bert's life and we asked four serving and former politicians to participate. In a very real sense, John Hyde was Bert Kelly's successor in parliament. Like Kelly, Hyde was a farmer and learned the lessons well from him and went on, like Bert, to become a national newspaper columnist.

Gough Whitlam, Prime Minister from 1972-75, broke the protectionist mould that had shaped Australia's industrial landscape for most of this century, when his government cut tariffs by 25% in 1973. In his remarks, Mr Whitlam said that 'no private member has had as much influence in changing a major policy of the major parties'.

David Kemp, currently a Minister in the Howard government, during 1996 was the second politician to deliver a lecture in the Centre's Bert Kelly Lectures, the first being Labor frontbencher Mark Latham. Dr Kemp had been a friend of Bert Kelly's for many years and as is clear from his remarks, Kelly was a considerable influence on his thinking.

The function was chaired by Jim Carlton, a former Federal Health Minister and now Director General of the Australian Red Cross, but when in parliament, like Bert, a courageous fighter for sound economic policy.

Journalism too played a major role in Bert's life and Paul Kelly, one of Australia's senior journalists, joined the speakers. In describing Bert

Kelly as a modern thinker and an old-fashioned politician he gave us one of the most perceptive descriptions of the man. Finally his long-time friend Ray Evans brought us a very clear picture of the moral underpinnings that drove Bert's thinking and action.

Nevertheless, good ideas will always find themselves under challenge and that seems to be the case at present and from various parts of the political and ideological spectrum. As Paul Kelly asked is there some sort of collective amnesia at work? Have we forgotten the past already? Is the economic nationalism being proposed as old and as dangerous to our prosperity as what we have seen for too much of our history? The ideas that Bert stood for will need restating and reinforcing if Australia is to remain a dynamic and forward-looking society. The lessons that Bert Kelly taught us also remind us that the way of bringing down bad ideas is by constantly putting forward the best ideas with hard work, patience and, if possible, humour. In particular, the 'protectionist snake', to use the words of Czech Prime Minister Václav Klaus, needs slaying again, and again, and again.

To me personally, Bert was an inspiration. The way he conducted his life was something that I would hope all aspire too and my friendship with Bert and Lorna was something that I will always treasure. At the Centre's 20th Anniversary last November, Bert was made one of the first ten Distinguished Fellows of the Centre. This was one way that the CIS could recognise the commitment of this remarkable man to the cause of liberty. The publication of this modest volume is another.

Greg Lindsay

John Hyde

Mr Chairman, members of Bert's family, ladies and gentlemen. As many of you will know, throughout nearly all of my political career, such as it was, I saw myself and was seen by others as Bert Kelly's acolyte. He taught me nothing more important than the moral dimensions of politics. He taught me by example and exhortation that, difficult as I may find being morally bound to the service of all present and future Australians, that so long as I remained an MP, I was so bound. That is, no faction of party, professions, industry, class, race or sex ought to divert me from the interest of the whole. And no inducement by way of preferment, praise, votes or honours or any ridicule ought to silence me in pursuit of the long term Australian interest. Such heavy responsibility and such Puritan ethics might have taken most of the fun out of politics, but it didn't.

Of course, I failed. I reckon even Kelly failed sometimes, but he less than any man I knew. I respect him and indeed loved him, and I deem it a great honour to have been asked to speak at this tribute to Bert Kelly. It is my responsibility tonight to discuss his use of the office of parliamentarian.

I begin by reminding you of Edmund Burke's oft quoted letter to the citizens of Bristol:

> Parliament is not a congress of ambassadors from different
> and hostile interests; which interests each must maintain, as
> agent and advocate, against other agents and advocates; but
> parliament is a deliberative assembly of one nation, with one
> interest, that of the whole; where not local purposes or lo-
> cal prejudices ought to guide, but the general good, result-

---

John Hyde was a member of the House of Representatives
from 1974 to 1983.

ing from the general reason of the whole. You choose a member indeed; but when you have chosen him, he is not a member of Bristol but a member of parliament.

Burke's preference for the interests of the whole of one nation, which he most courageously defended, is left too little room in today's parliaments in which fealty is accorded not only to the vested interests within individual members' electorates but also to political parties and even their factions. Where the best organised lobbies demand and receive the privilege of legislation that applies, not to everyone, but to people of a race, sex, association or industry.

St Matthew forecast the consequences of split allegiance as well as anyone:

No man can serve two master: for either he will hate the one and love the other' or else he will hold to one and despise the other.

Politics can be a bitter pastime – note the pillorying of Senator Colston that seems to motivated by everything but ethical standards. I never heard Bert, even in private conversation, yield to bitterness or indulge in vengeance.

The party system can, for those not as given to tribal loyalty as Senator Ray, instead be soporific.

W.S. Gilbert better described many modern MPs then did Burke.

I always voted at my party's call

And never thought of thinking for myself at all

When an inexperienced backbencher in Federal Opposition, I made a speech lambasting your Government, Mr Whitlam, for the then high nominal interest rates. My difficulty was that inflation was well into double figures, real rates were negative, and, to remedy the damage, even higher rates were required. Later that day, Bert Kelly chose a chair beside me in the members' dining room. 'Did you believe that nonsense you mouthed in the House this morning?' 'No', I said, 'but the whip....' 'Why say it?' I still smart from the admonition.

The great commentator on the British Constitution, Walter Bagehot, described five functions of the House of Commons and, by implication, any Westminster parliamentary lower chamber. These were:

The elective function: He said 'it is the assembly that chooses our president'.

It fills this function well and I know of no evidence that Kelly played a decisive or exceptional role in choosing or trying to prevent the choice of Menzies, Holt, Gorton, McMahon, Whitlam, Snedden or Fraser. He was not a numbers man.

I do remember him telling the party room that if he were to campaign in the Bass by-election, he would be 'on Gough's side'. In hindsight, I am prepared to tell the world that the argument the Coalition was employing in Bass was a pack of lies. What made Bert exceptional was that he alone was game to tell the party room at the time.

The expressive: 'it expresses the mind of the people on matters that come before it.'

Parliament has far too much government business before it for Members to get the Speaker's call when they want it, but MPs have other, sometimes better, opportunities to demonstrate the art of followship.

The teaching function: Bagehot had this to say: 'A great open council of considerable men cannot be placed in the middle of society without altering that society. It ought alter it for the better. It ought to teach the nation what it does not know.'

One cannot read those words without thinking of Bert and of the arts of leadership which are surely about making what is unpopular, popular; what is unacceptable, acceptable. Any lightweight can lead kids into a lolly shop: Bert led them out! More of how he went about it in a moment.

Bagehot's other two functions were:

The informing function: petitions and all that.

And *the legislative function* which Bagehot said was, except in rare seasons, less important than executive management (which is obviously true) or the teaching function of parliament (which in a discussion of Bert's career is interesting). Over a century ago Bagehot thought that governments were furnished with too much that was too specific in its application. I wonder what he would make of today's statute book?

By proceeding as though Parliament is what it is supposed to be and its name implies, that is an organisation dedicated to discovery by debate, Kelly gave it that character. By proceeding as though it was axiomatic that its members should serve all Australians without favour, rather than the factions of industry, trade and profession, he shamed some into governing in that manner. Time and again, when naked factional interest paraded as national interest, it was Bert who first noted that an Emperor of the day wore no clothes.

It is timely that we should be reviewing Bert Kelly's career now when the exploitive face – the ugly face – of capitalism is again being shown to Australians. I am not now thinking of felonies such as misappropriating shareholders' property to build houses, acquire Van Goghs or finance horse studs any more than I was thinking of travel allowances when I observed that Bert identified the moral dimensions of politics. Society knows more or less how to deal with simple crooks. I am more concerned by the ability of those with access to corporate treasure chests to mount campaigns for government-mandated largess in the form of higher than free market prices. It is a form of corruption that is more dangerous to the ambient society than is stealing half a house.

It is appropriate that we be reminded of Bert when we again have a Government that is showing signs of maintaining the privileges of groups with political clout and an Opposition that has made it quite clear that it has abandoned the resolve of the Hawke and Keating Governments to open the Australian economy. When we have a Minister for Industry who is apparently more than willing to use public authority to serve private interests, and pre-empts Cabinet solidarity, we are returning to the days and methods of John McEwen.

Again we hear the siren call of industrial favouritism that can be enjoyed only at the expense of other Australians. Again we hear disingenuous misuse of the level playing field metaphor. It insists only that Australian governments treat all Australians equally. To demand that Australian governments treat Australians unequally to very selectively match the follies of other nations is to stand it on its head. When a car or textile manufacturer calls for the level of protection for Australian wheat growers that the European Union wheat farmers already enjoy then I'll respect his integrity, if not his economic acumen. He won't do that, however, because he already knows that farmers' protection would result in lower living standards for everyone including manufacturers, just as farmers and miners now pay for car and textile tariffs.

Bert taught us that one Australian's tariff is another Australian's job. He taught us that welfare is for people, not industries. He insisted, rightly, that there is no such thing as a free lunch. Above all he taught us to recognise and oppose privilege because privilege is wrong.

The forums that Bert employed to give effect to the educative function of parliament, the Hansard, media reports, speeches and even the occasional newspaper column, though probably not a regular column, are available to any MP. If I, at Bert's insistence, can teach myself to write a column anybody can. Very few, indeed nobody that I can think of, made such effective use of these opportunities as did Bert. Why Kelly?

First: Hard work. Credibility is everything to anyone who would persuade another to change his mind. There is thus no substitute for getting both the facts and the argument right not just sometimes. Bert sat up late teaching himself from the standard texts the theories that economists have developed concerning the circumstances that will advance what Burke called 'the general good'. He sat up many many more nights reading Tariff Board and IAC reports and the reports of relevant committees and bodies such as the OECD that are based on those theories. He wrote the relevant arguments down in the form of newspaper columns checking them, as one does, against slips in fact or argument, careless overstatement or too sweeping generality. Having got his arguments right, he did not hesitate to recycle them, however. In public life accuracy is a much greater virtue than originality.

Second: He used expert advice. When he did not know, he did not hesitate to ask. In this, an MP has a considerable advantage over most people. There are very many experts in academe and, within the bounds of propriety, the civil service, who are more than willing to devote patient hours to assisting any parliamentarian whom they feel really is trying to advance 'the general good'.

Third: An heir to the traditions of nineteenth century British liberalism, he opposed all privilege and was remarkably consistent in both the economic and the social spheres. His eye firmly fixed on 'the general good', he used the moral high ground to great effect and his humour sometimes sorely punished particularly those politicians who cosied up to vested interests.

Fourth: He was courageous. Today, his name is associated with a campaign that is, in spite of current signs backsliding, largely won – at least at the level of debate. Those of us who were close to him in politics, however, would have respected and loved him as much, if he had failed. We understood enough to appreciate the fortitude required to stand alone on behalf of 'the general good' in the parliament and party room and we gained an inkling of the strength he needed to withstand public ridicule that persisted for considerably more than a decade. A few billion dollars of government favours finances a lot of ridicule.

Fifth: He did not allow his own preferment to get in the way of his duty to 'the general good'. I had the honour of seeing Kelly defend the IAC against emasculation by the Fraser Government. I use 'honour' advisedly. He was the epitome of Australian civic virtue: as one who brought to the office of Federal Parliamentarian prescience, clear-sightedness, determination, wit, and above all a form of courage that was so rare as to be nearly exceptional.

All these advantages are available to any MP who has the fortitude to claim them. In conclusion, I briefly mention three advantages that were his alone but which all contributed to his success.

First: He was lovable and lovable people are rightly accorded a special hearing.

Second: There was Lorna his helpmate and sternest critic. Anyone who had the good fortune to marry a Lorna would be a bloody fool to neglect the advantage.

Third: He had a facility with the pen that was, I know, carefully cultivated by the aforementioned hard work but which was, I suspect, also partly innate.

Thus, apart from his facility with the pen, Bert Kelly's strengths were more moral than intellectual. He had little aptitude for the power of princes and achieved little during his brief period in the ministry. A less Machiavellian character never served in the Federal Parliament. Nevertheless, no history of the economy or the parliament should omit his achievements.

E. G. Whitlam

I was asked to this congregation because I turned up at Bert Kelly's funeral in Adelaide on 24 January last. There were some moving but joyful tributes by Bert's family and friends. An excellent formal eulogy was delivered by Ray Evans. On 17 February Ray left a message for me to phone him at Western Mining. I had not been asked to contact anyone at that outfit since I opened its new place at Kalgoorlie in April 1973. Ray told me that he was inviting me to this function to be organised by the Centre for Independent Studies in his capacity as president of the H. R. Nicholls Society. I warily inquired who else was being invited. He mentioned some names. Molière's words came to mind: Que diable allais-je faire dans cette galère? What the devil was I doing in that crew?

For greater precaution I later asked Greg Lindsay who would be taking the chair. Among the persons, all male, being considered was Jim Carlton. I first knew of him when he was Secretary of the New South Wales branch of the Liberal Party. He is now national secretary of the Australian Red Cross. Approving his passage from the promotion to the resolution of conflict, I told Greg that, if Jim was Chairperson, I would happily join in a tribute to Bert Kelly. On 26 February he wrote to confirm the deal. To my astonishment, I later learned that on the same day New Labor was conjuring up New Protection, a ghost from the past, not from the age of McEwen or Scullin but Deakin. (Deakin, Scullin, McEwen and I were all born in Victoria.)

I decided to stay on course. In my innocence I had thought I would belatedly be making a nostalgic but genuine tribute to Bert Kelly, as many others had done when Parliament reconvened. Knowing that there

---

Gough Whitlam was Prime Minister of Australia from 1972 to 1975.

were no Labor members from Kelly's time I had suggested some lines to Kim Beazley, my successor.

No private member has had as much influence in changing a major policy of the major parties.

From his father W.S. (Stan) Kelly OBE, a member of the Tariff Board from 1929 to 1940, Bert imbibed a deep scepticism about the Scullin Government's policy of tariffs on request. McEwen hated him. I thought that Kelly's speeches on Tariff Board reports were much more consistently rational than those of his colleagues or my colleagues. I naturally approved his support for my Government's 25 per cent tariff cuts in 1973.

During the Bass by-election in 1975, which is often compared with the Canberra by-election in 1995, the Liberals blamed the tariff cuts for the decline of the textile industry in Launceston. At Friday's exuberant wake several Liberals enjoyed recalling that Fraser had urged Kelly to campaign in Bass. Kelly responded that he was intending to do so – for me.

The State Funeral was held at Wesley Uniting Church at Kent Town. The congregation audibly approved when the officiating minister carefully enunciated the name of the first hymn 'They who tread the Path of Labour'.

Bert Kelly was christened Charles Robert after his maternal and paternal grandfathers. The congregation still more audibly approved when Bert's eldest son explained the order; W.S Kelly was not going to have an R.C. Kelly in his family.

I also quote from the condolence speech by the next speaker today, David Kemp:

> Now, after several decades of Bert's influence, we recognise
> that there are very few jobs in the Australian economy still
> dependent upon tariffs. The jobs that are coming into exist-
> ence at the moment are jobs which can stand on their own
> in the global economy. Australia is stronger and more se-
> cure as a result. We have Bert Kelly to thank for that.

I assume that David is one of the members who will keep his own side on track. As a modest ex-member I must do my best to get my own side back on track.

First, however, may I give some background to my abiding esteem for Bert Kelly. I did not know Stan Kelly but after I left Canberra for the University of Sydney in the mid-30s, my parents and my sister came to know him well through another South Australian, Stan Jackson, the Commissioner for Taxation. Stan Jackson was a great friend and the best client of my father, the Crown Solicitor. The three men were all born in 1884. Joe Lyons headed but did not run the Government and Kelly was not a common name in the top departments. My mother used to recall that Stan was a Kelly from the Isle of Man.

Australians now accept that the fate of legislation in the National Parliament depends on the whims of two senators who sit on the cross benches, the Grand Inquisitor from Tasmania and the Grand Acquisitor from Queensland, both elected in 1975. The man to whom we are paying tribute sat on the back benches for all but three of his years in Parliament. Yet he had sufficient knowledge, skill, courage and persistence to reverse the policies of a powerful statesman who had been an MP for 36 years and five months – only two MPs and two senators have served longer – a cabinet minister for 26 years and Deputy Prime Minister for 13 years. I myself had great respect and affection for John McEwen, but I thought he was wrong. I treasure his statement about my parents and me in his last speech in Parliament in October 1970.

On 27 September 1973, as a result of what I myself learned from Bert Kelly, Sir John Crawford and Nugget Coombs, I introduced the bill for the Industries Assistance Commission to replace the Tariff Board established in 1921. I emphasised the clause 'which states that the Government shall not take any action to provide assistance to a particular industry until it has received a report on the matter from the Commission'. At this point *Hansard* records two interjections:

Mr Street: *Hear, hear!*
Mr Kelly: *Hear, hear!*

A decade later Tony Street was succeeded as MP for Corangamite by Stewart McArthur, whose presence at the funeral, speech in Parliament and presence today I have enjoyed.

The Federal Opposition is now being incited to subvert the process which the Parliament enacted in 1973. Last August Treasurer Costello asked the Industry Commission, now being renamed the Productivity Commission, to report on Australia's automotive industry. (I must correct the impression that the new title was the idea of the founding father of the Lyons Forum, Chris Miles, who introduced the bill. The title was used by John Howard in a headland speech in July 1995. It turned out to be a core promise.) An issues paper announced:

Following receipt of submissions, the Commission will prepare and release a draft report in late December 1996. Interested parties will then have an opportunity to make further submissions and to comment on the draft report at a round of public hearings in Adelaide, Melbourne and Sydney. These public hearings will be held in February/March 1997. The Commission will then prepare its final report and present it to the Federal Government by 12 May 1997.

The Federal Opposition did not make submissions to the commission. After the draft report was released in late December, it still did not make submissions to the Commission. It made submissions last year to the Industrial Relations Commission at its public hearings on the basic wage case. Why did it not make submissions to the Productivity Commission at its public hearings in Adelaide, Melbourne and Sydney last month or this? It did not wait for the final report due by 12 May. Instead an announcement was made at an automotive trim plant in Adelaide on 26 February preempting the Commission's final report. Existing plans ensure that automotive tariffs will be down to 15 per cent in the year 2000. The so-called Labor plan proposes that the tariff should be frozen at 15 per cent until at least 2005. Labor would review the position in 2003 to determine what assistance would be needed beyond 2005 having regard to the progress of our trading partners in achieving the APEC forum tariff reduction targets.

Regional populism is not even good politics. Labor lost one seat in Victoria and two in South Australia at the Federal elections a year ago. It did not lose them because tariffs might fall after 2000. Labor lost 13 seats in NSW and 11 in Queensland. It won't win them back by promising to freeze tariffs after 2000. Voters in NSW, Queensland, Western Australia and Tasmania now know that tariffs are a hidden tax on the vehicles that individuals and corporations have to buy.

I am sure that the views of most Australians, including Labor voters, are expressed in the supplementary submission which the NRMA made on the draft report in February. I quote from it:

> The Australian consumer has benefited considerably from the industry's increasing exposure to international competition. Quality and choice are now far superior to what they were 10 years ago when the Australian industry was inward-looking and devoid of incentive to achieve best practice. The momentum of these reforms should be carried forward as quickly as possible after the year 2000... We do not consider that the argument that further cuts be contingent on reciprocal measures taken by other APEC economies is persuasive, or that it is a winning strategy for consumers... The commission's report notes that the cost to consumers of current tariff levels is, on average, $3,700 per vehicle, which reduces to $2,100 per vehicle in the year 2000 when the

prevailing rate of tariff protection will be 15%... The NRMA agrees with the recommendation that tariffs on micro/light passenger motor vehicles be reduced to five per cent from 1 January 2001, if not sooner.

The internationalisation of the Australian economy began with my Government's 25 per cent across-the-board tariff cut of July 1973. It seemed to me that companies, very often foreign companies, were setting up industries in Australia in the confidence that, however uneconomic the industries turned out to be, governments would always ensure sufficient protection to keep the industries afloat. I also saw the burden which protection for some industries imposed on other industries which did not receive or need protection. Those industries which would never be able to provide products for Australian consumers as cheaply as they could get the products from overseas were compelling other industries to charge prices which made their products unnecessarily expensive for the customers in Australia and which put their products out of the reach of customers overseas.

In Australia the 1973 tariff cut ended an ethos of protection all-round which took its antecedents from the time of Scullin. McEwen used the tariff wall to establish a system of protection-on-demand. For decades this imposed a high flat tax on consumers. It was no less damaging to living standards than a GST. Even today Australians are forced to pay an additional $3,000, on average, for the purchase of a new car.

It is sometimes argued that tariffs protect jobs and foster employment security. They do not. History tells us that the industries which lost most jobs and discarded most workers in Australia were those most protected by tariffs and quotas. Profits in the same industries were always well above average. Protection has always protected profits, not jobs.

There are three basic reasons why tariffs have failed to secure employment in protected industries. First, the most heavily protected industries are the most inefficient ones and thereby the least able to adapt to new situations. Secondly, protection in Australia has been afforded to industries which aim only to serve our small domestic market. Investment expenditure then becomes a means – not for the development of new products or increasing production – but simply for replacing workers with new, automated technologies. Thirdly, during an era in which capital is increasingly footloose, protection and subsidies in one nation might be overtaken by other nations also bidding for capital investment.

Just as States and Territories in Australia do not serve the national interest by bidding against each other and over-subsidising business, Australians are not well served by national governments which engage in the folly of tariff protection. Shielding capital from competition is not an effective way for the nation-state to exercise leverage over the mobility of investment. Tariff walls and subsidies do not prevent capital from relocating to other nations offering even more generous protection. Bidding wars between national jurisdictions do not favour nations and their workers, but the interests of footloose investment and profit maximisation. They do not deliver job security, properly understood and enjoyed, but merely short term relief from the chase of capital across the globe. The only security workers can have in an open economy is a set of high value added skills for which the private sector is willing to pay an international premium.

The leverage of the nation-state relies on two related strategies. The first is to foster economic multilateralism between nations. This is the principle by which the Chifley Government committed itself to the Bretton Woods system. It is the principle by which the Hawke and Keating Governments advanced the virtues of free trade and investment in the Asia-Pacific region under the banner of APEC. It is part of a Labor tradition dating from the end of World War II. Just as capital has lifted its sphere of activity to a global level, so too must nations. It makes sense to respond to economic internationalisation by internationalising the means by which governments exercise their regulatory powers and influence. This is the approach, for instance, which has made the European Union a stronger force in the world economy. It is an approach which Australian Labor – by tradition as well as commonsense strategy – must always embrace.

Bilateralism never works as well in international affairs as multilateralism. There can be no more constructive force than nations working in large number to promote the rights of citizens for social freedoms, labour standards and the free movement of trade and investment. This approach should not be reduced to a narrow focus on bilateralism and reciprocity. In trade policy, reciprocity is simply a recipe for doing nothing. The advocates quote St Augustine's Confessions: 'make me chaste and continent, but not yet'. It is estimated that unilateral tariff reform has the potential to add $4 billion per annum to Australia's economic output.

A second strategy for dealing with footloose capital lies in education policy. In an open economy the true wealth of a nation and its capacity to exercise economic leverage lies in the skills of its people. Labour and the value it adds to the production process is the only immobile factor of production. Hence, it is the only means by which the nation-state can engineer economic activity according to national interests, rather than the interests of footloose capital. Experiences in successful economies show that capital is willing to chase a well educated and highly skilled workforce. This generates a growing share of employment in the traded sector. Increased spending power by high skill, high value-added workers, in turn, creates new jobs in the non-traded sector of the national economy. This transmission effect between workforce skills and the traded and non-traded sectors is the key to full employment in an open economy. It is the correct path to economic nationalism. It makes footloose capital chase nations and their skills, rather than the reverse. It allows workers to enjoy the benefits of internationally competitive skills and employment growth.

One of the problems with the protectionist road is that it drains the resources a nation might otherwise allocate to education and training. Industry protection by definition allocates resources to less efficient economic activities, thereby draining national income growth. It also collects a flat tax on expenditure, thereby limiting the resources people might otherwise direct toward education and training.

For the Labor Party this approach is particularly damaging. It is unsatisfactory enough for the Howard Government to be reducing the capacity of Australia's universities, TAFE system and schools to produce scholars and skilled workers. Now Labor in Opposition appears to be wanting to direct scarce public resouces to a re-run of Scullinism and McEwenism. Our Party should have no more important objective than the skills of each generation of Australian workers. Our appeal to the Australian electorate should not be based on propping up the profits of smokestack industries, but on fostering the growth of high skill, high value added, well paid jobs throughout the Australian economy. Regional populism should not be allowed to substitute for the virtues of social mobility and national economic leverage.

There is nothing in the traditions of the modern Labor Party which endorses industry protection. Now is not the time to wind back the achievements of the last three Labor Governments – Whitlam, Hawke and Keating – in the internationalisation of the economy. Labor has spent a decade or more lampooning John Howard for living in the past on social policy. Now is not the time for Labor to go back to the past on trade and industry policy.

David Kemp

T he slot I fill this evening is that of the current politician on Bert's own side of politics. This is a signal honour, because Bert spent a great deal of his time trying to educate his Liberal colleagues, and I was certainly the recipient of his good advice as I shall tell.

It is not often that one has the opportunity to honour someone who was a genuine leader of opinion in relation to one of the truly remarkable shifts in Australian policy. While there were others whose contributions were significant, it was Bert who carried the fight against tariff protection into the parliamentary arena at a time when conventional wisdom was strongly on the other side. Until Bert Kelly, tariff protection was a 'settled' policy. After Bert Kelly, it was distinctly unsettled.

I first met Bert Kelly during the 1970s when he was already notorious as a relentless, if self-deprecating, opponent of tariff protection. I was predisposed to like him immediately because, from my days as a student of history at Melbourne University, I had already made the acquaintance of his British forebears, Richard Cobden and John Bright, in collections of documents in the Baillieu Library, and had been convinced of the merits of free trade by the arguments of the Manchester School.

Those free traders, like Bert, were highly effective on the public platform and in changing national policy.

I do not recall, however, that any of them used humour quite so effectively as Bert Kelly in revealing the flaws in his opponents' arguments. Bert seized every opportunity to do so. After the 1976 Melbourne Cup, won by a New Zealand horse, he quickly thought up a question for the relevant Minister:

David Kemp is Minister for Schools, Vocational Education and Training

Because of the consistently strong competition from New Zealand, will the Minister see what can be done to put a tariff on New Zealand horses in order to prevent them running faster than our home produced horses?

This brought the House down.

He did not use his wit only against tariffs. On one occasion he asked Jim Cairns as Treasurer:

Last week the Treasurer told us about his policy of using deficit financing to lower the present level of unemployment. How is this solution of burying the unemployment problem under a mountain of money actually working out? If printing money is a good solution for the unemployment problem, why not print more of the stuff and get rid of the unemployment problem altogether?

Kelly recalled:

And Jim Cairns, with his kind heart brimming over with love and affection, just could not resist agreeing with me and replied that that was just what the government had in mind.

Many keen political observers pinpoint the beginning of Cairns' decline from that reply.

In 1981, when I was Director of the Prime Minister's Office, Bert presented me with a copy of a collection of his columns entitled *Economics Made Easy*. In it he included a note which I only rediscovered earlier this week. It read:

'If you think it is worth $5 send a cheque. If not, try leaving it around for the P.M. to see.'

I did both.

Going back to my university days in the 1960s I still remember vividly debates with fellow students, many of whom could not believe that anyone would support such an out-of-date doctrine as free trade, when it had been so soundly and roundly defeated in Australian political battles during the first decade of this century. Little did any of us realise that we were already living in the sunset days of the era of protection all round, and that one of the most basic of the so-called 'settled policies' of Australian politics (along with centralised arbitration) was about to be overturned– and Bert Kelly was to have no mean role in this development.

The arguments of the old free traders remain to me very convincing. They were arguments not merely of self-interest on behalf of the efficient textile manufacturers represented by the Manchester School, but they were arguments with a strong moral foundation, and they were arguments very appropriate to the dawning age of democracy with its belief in the rights of every person to live under laws which applied equally to all.

It was plain that in nineteenth century Britain as in late twentieth century Australia the arguments for tariff protection, however clothed in the rhetoric of protecting tradition, community and jobs, were arguments for privileges and special benefits for one section of the community at the expense of everybody else. In nineteenth century England it was probably clearer that tariffs were to protect a particular class structure than in more recent times, but that is also true of more recent arguments.

Of all the arguments then, as now, undoubtedly the one with the most political impact was that free trade was in the interests of those on lowest incomes in the community, because it was they who benefited most from lower prices for corn, or clothes, or shoes or whatever. Bert Kelly frequently used simple calculations of the differences between the costs of bed sheets or cars to the consumer to demonstrate that even the consumer whose main concern was to keep one jump ahead of the finance companies also had an interest in getting tariffs down.

The consumer interest, fortunately, still provides a strong and appealing argument, even if it is not always successful on the day.

The argument that really intrigued me, however, when I first heard it – and is still of fundamental importance today, was the claim that free trade was closely associated with international peace. It was a belief that made the free traders anti-imperialist in their day – and they lost that argument at the time, when the world was dividing up into empires that were soon to be at each other's throats. Bert was not slow to remind his readers that the high tariff barriers established by the USA and Europe against Japan 'was the beginning of World War II as far as Japan was concerned'. His particular concern was that at one point we were putting up barriers against our Asian neighbours with whom it was particularly important to be friendly. 'If we refuse to buy from our neighbours we clearly hurt them, but we also hurt ourselves'.

Free traders are equally the opponents of trading blocks today, and that is an argument which can surely still be won.

There are those on the scene who would argue that support for free trade arises from some otherworldly theory quite out of touch with the real world. This is the reverse of the truth. The arguments for freer trade are compelling because they recognise a number of fundamental realities of life:

- that you do not promote an industry effectively by increasing the price of its products;

- that we cannot make ourselves better off by impoverishing our potential customers;

- that competition breeds efficiency and government protected monopolies breed exploitation;

- that we diminish our wealth by wasting resources on things others can do better; and

- that policies based on choice generally satisfy more people than any alternative.

It was Bert Kelly's great strength that he embodied in his own life and manner the sheer irrepressible commonsense and moral strength of the free market position. When he had done a few simple calculations and exposed the absurdity of his opponents' claims with a few deft strokes of the pen, no one could doubt that he was completely in touch with the real world and not an ideological exponent of some ivory-tower doctrine.

The tariff debate is largely won. In relation to the remaining protected industries the issue is one of the pace of change rather than the direction. The Government is committed to the APEC goal of trade liberalisation by the year 2010, and is maintaining the existing schedule of tariff reductions over the next three years. It is good to be able to record tonight the decision announced last week to bring to an end tariff protection of the sugar industry from 1 July this year.

As the global economy advances inexorably, and as we move towards the more complete implementation of the principles of liberal trade, we can indeed see the extraordinary impact of the forces of freer trade on the prosperity of the countries in our own region of the world – where huge middle classes are now emerging in Southeast and East Asia, in India and China. These middle classes are not only wealthier consumers of Australia's exports. They are also the foundations on which successful political liberalisation can occur in countries which have never before known stable democratic institutions.

Bert Kelly always made it clear that while so much of his attention was given to the tariff question, his conclusions on tariff policy were but a straightforward deduction from recognising the significance of the laws of supply and demand. As he said in his inimitable way in an essay I enjoyed at the time it was published in 1979 and still enjoy:

I do not defend the law of supply and demand. Even Eccles

is a bit ashamed that it is called an economic law, because it certainly has its ruthless aspects. Perhaps it would be nice to have a more gentle law in its place though I admit it is hard to think how one would work. But while the law is in force, we should either recognise and in the end obey it, or get the wretched thing rescinded. But for goodness sake don't let's pretend it isn't there and go round kidding people and even ourselves that we can increase the price of goods and services without decreasing the demand for them. This may get us votes, but it doesn't help get rid of unemployment.

Australia today had better heed his message. We are a country which remains vulnerable. We can be dynamic, vibrant, strong and prosperous – and we will be if we continue to have the courage to push ahead with the reform agenda which is implicit in recognition of the basic commonsense principles for which Bert Kelly was such an effective advocate.

N. R. Evans

We have been reminded in recent days that the debate over protectionism is never over. I had thought that back in September 1992, when the car makers ran a very vigorous campaign, aimed in the first instance to break the Coalition in opposition, but which was in reality designed ultimately to force the Keating Government to resile from its phase-out policy on tariffs, that in winning that battle the anti-protectionists had won a victory which would secure the field for at least a decade. Four and a half years later the Coalition, which in opposition held firm, is now dithering in government. The Labor Party which in government in 1992 ultimately (when it became clear that the Opposition would not break) held the line, has now decided to beat up the Coalition on an issue which, when they were in government, is arguably the most significant thing they did.

That particular story demonstrates how powerful the Opposition really is. It is the Opposition which defines the parameters within which a government feels comfortable, and that is particularly true of a government like the present Government, which follows rather than leads.

So now we are back into the protectionist debate and Bert is no longer with us to give advice and urge us on. I do miss his telephone calls and his cheerful encouragement. At a time then when he is missed the question arises why was Bert so successful as a preacher? – a word I use advisedly.

At least part of the answer was that he had absorbed as a boy and a young man the exegetical techniques of the Methodist preacher. It is not widely known that John Wesley and the early Methodists were strong adherents of free trade, although they had no scruples in applying their

---

Ray Evans is Executive Officer of Western Mining.

own trade sanctions when they deemed such measures appropriate. Wesley, for example, urged his followers to eschew sugar because West Indian sugar was grown with slave labour and the Methodists were strong supporters of the abolitionist movement. When the attention of the free traders was later focused on the corn laws and the anti-corn law league was established, the Methodists provided a large proportion of the rank and file. The repeal of the Corn Laws in 1846 was in large measure due to the unswerving Methodist support, over many years, for the anti-corn law league.

There were a number of different strains of Methodism. Cornish Methodism, which dominated the mining industry, tended to great enthusiasm and emotional display. Manxian Methodism, from the Isle of Man from whence the Kellys arrived in Adelaide in 1838, was more cerebral, but regardless of which particular faction or tradition was prevalent in a particular place, Methodism was based on the Bible and the Methodist Hymn Book, and in Bible teaching the parables which Jesus used to illustrate his doctrines concerning, for example, the Kingdom of Heaven, are paramount.

The Oxford English Dictionary defines 'parable' as a narrative of imagined events used to typify moral or spiritual relations. I am not completely happy with that definition in that the incidents described in the parables are usually the stuff of real experience, although they may be given an unexpected twist. They are indeed successful because they speak of life either as we have experienced it, or as we can easily imagine it to be. Bert's parables were not imagined, they were examples of rural and political life which he used to illustrate a moral reality.

His most famous parable is, I think, the parable of the young bull. A young, energetic bull, full of bounce and confidence, comes bounding into the cow yard and races straight up to a demure and much smaller cow. To the astonishment of the observer, (particularly an urban observer) instead of leaping over the cow to perform his conjugal duties, the young bull gets down on his haunches, and gets his huge head up into the foster cow's udder, and begins sucking away for dear life.

With this incident from rural life Bert demolished the infant industry argument for protection, and the example of the overgrown young bull which he usually cited was BHP.

BHP in those days was a divided house on the protectionist issue. The steel division believed it benefited from protection and the minerals division suspected it was disadvantaged. But Ian McLennan came down on the protectionist side and the free-traders within had to run a guerilla campaign. Bert's parable must have been a godsend to them.

Another typical example of a Bert Kelly parable is the story of the unimpressed farmer. For reasons which may have originated in theological disputation around the dinner table at Merrindie, the farmer in this story was an adherent of Rome, and one day he was showing the parish priest around the farm. It was a beautiful spring day and the grass was high and lush, the stock were looking superb, the fences were in good shape, and the priest was duly impressed. 'Well Pat' said the priest, 'between you and God, the pair of you have done a great job on this place.' The farmer was totally unimpressed. 'I dunno about that Father' he replied, 'You should have seen this place when God had it all to himself.'

Bert constantly worked on these parables, refining them and tailoring them to suit different situations as only a real professional can.

The Bible was an obvious source of reference and of exegetical method. Kipling was another major influence. Reading aloud after dinner with the aid of a kerosene lamp was the evening's entertainment at Merrindie and by the time he went to Prince Alfred, Bert had much of Kipling's poetry committed to memory. Kipling is seen by many today as the poet of the British Raj, which is true in one sense, but can be entirely misleading in another. Malcolm Muggeridge regarded Kipling as the greatest writer of his generation and I suspect his works are still selling well. I have always assumed it is no accident that Bert and Lorna's second son is called Kim.

A delightful vignette of family life which Bert's younger sister Marion related to me describes dinner at Merrindie during the time when WS was in Melbourne attending to his Tariff Board duties, his wife Ada who divided her time between Merrindie and Melbourne was in Melbourne, and Winifred, the eldest, was deputising for her mother. Bert had just assumed responsibility for working the farm and there must have been some sort of power struggle as to who was really in charge. Dinner had been served to everyone except Bert when Winifred said grace, after which Bert announced sternly albeit respectfully, 'Not me, O Lord'.

It takes genius to produce a parable with the power of the story of the young bull. Today the argument on protection is centred on reciprocity. Why should we reduce our protection unless our neighbours in the Asia-Pacific region reduce theirs. The Prime Minister, and the former Federal President of the Liberal Party, John Elliott, have made common cause in arguing this case. Bert Kelly was not able to kill this argument with a parable comparable to that of the young bull. He did however put me on to a marvellous example of ministerial endorsement of the doctrine which is worth relating this evening.

Doug Anthony, who was Deputy Prime Minister and Minister for Trade, returned from taking part in the Multilateral Trade Negotiations which ultimately led to the Uruguay Agreement, reported on his adventures to the House of Representatives on 20 September 1979. He explained to the House

> What are negotiations of this nature? They are negotiations by Australia to seek certain benefits such as access to markets at the lowest possible price. Although we have to give concessions, naturally we want to keep them as minimal as possible. By the same token we want to achieve our objectives of lower tariffs round the world and of getting access to markets...

He concluded his remarks thus:

> Not one single tariff will be reduced. There has been no reduction at all in industrial tariffs. Honourable members must acclaim that we have done a magnificent job in our negotiations when we have come out of them without having to pay anything more than making a binding on industrial tariffs. [The term 'binding' means a commitment to freeze tariff at current levels].

The model which informs Doug Anthony's remarks is one which is widely held – and that is that the most favourable position which a country can hold in international trading relations is one in which the rest of the world is committed entirely to free trade, but that we are highly protectionist. The logical extension of this idea is that the best of all possible worlds for Australia is a world in which we have huge exports and no imports. This was the original form of mercantilist doctrine in which the primary, if not the sole, objective in international trade, was to build up huge inventories of gold bullion.

This doctrine has, for centuries, enjoyed wide support. Because of this widely held belief the whole of the GATT enterprise, since 1947, has been based upon parallel negotiations between all of the members, in which a tit for tat process enables them to lower trade barriers at home, in exchange for other members lowering theirs, as part of an all embracing deal, in which everyone moves more or less together. But the painful part of the process was trying to ensure that whatever part of one's own trade barriers was given up, was more than compensated by trade barriers given up by others. It also produced the perverse result that those nations which started out with minimum trade barriers were, in terms of the GATT negotiations, at a disadvantage.

The success of the Asian Tigers, particularly Hong Kong and Singapore, in achieving unprecedented rates of growth through a process of opening up their markets to the world has dented the hold which mercantilism exerts on people's thinking. But the killer argument, in my view, to any tariff, is the one which Bert pursued relentlessly throughout his career.

Bert was opposed to protectionism because it was wrong, and it was wrong because it created a situation in which governments, in the person of ministers or officials, granted arbitrary and capricious favours to some, who were thus greatly enriched, at the expense of others, who were at best impoverished and at worst, ruined. Bert was not really an economic rationalist as that term is now employed. Bert was the great embodiment of Edmund Burke's dictum that 'politics is morality writ large' and if the application of the moral principles which had been inculcated into him from childhood led to economically sensible conclusions, that was an additional benefit.

The stories he told to illustrate his arguments were drawn from life, not from textbooks, and they were informed by a well developed understanding of right and wrong, an understanding shaped by the Bible as well as by writers such as Kipling.

The simple answer, then, to those who are seeking a continuation of the tariff privileges which they have enjoyed for so long is that they are demanding the continuation of substantial financial benefits, at the expense of fellow citizens, which because they are necessarily arbitrary, and are therefore the fruits of energetic rent-seeking, cannot be justified. A tariff is a tax, paid by some and transferred immediately to others, without the authority of parliamentary scrutiny or budgetary appropriation. Tariffs do not create or protect jobs; they preserve some people's jobs at the expense of many more people who become jobless, or who can never get their foot on the employment ladder.

The Federal Treasurer has been heard in recent times to wax eloquent on the impropriety of corporate welfare. What comprises corporate welfare and what is the absence of ruinous taxation will always be cause for debate, but the essence of protectionism is that some are taxed, and others receive the proceeds of the tax. 'For he that hath, to him shall be given: and he that hath not, from him shall be taken away even that which he hath' (Mark 4:25) A tariff is the paradigm case of corporate welfare and I look forward to hearing the Treasurer taking part in this current debate on this issue.

In conclusion I wish to refer to the valedictory function that was organised at the Great Hall of the Art Gallery, here in Melbourne on 11 May 1988 to honour Bert after he was dropped as a columnist from *The Bulletin*. Bert was very disappointed at being dropped after 20 years as a columnist, so I thought that a valedictory occasion might temper his anguish.

It was an extraordinary evening. Over 400 people came from all over Australia, wearing decorations, and because they had come to pay tribute to Bert the occasion itself seemed to take on Bert's qualities. Laughter was continuous and at times even raucous. There were brief appreciations of Bert from Sir James Balderstone, Sir Arvi Parbo, Sir James Foots, and John Ralph. Then we had two main speeches, Bert himself and Alf Rattigan. Bert would often fall into the trap of mumbling a bit, and Alf Rattigan was always softly spoken, and the upshot was that for the best part of 50 minutes, subdued and rippling laughter completely overpowered the wisdom coming from the podium.

Bert was presented with a copper plaque on which was printed one of his 'modests' the description of Malcolm Fraser playing at King Canute, and two parliamentary questions; one on 7 November 1962, to John McEwen about the Tariff Board, which caused the Deputy Prime Minister to become extremely agitated, and the other to Treasurer Jim Cairn.

Soon after Dr Cairns was relieved of his portfolio and Bill Hayden was given the job of trying to sort out the mess.

That night in the Great Hall is remembered by many of those who attended as one of the happiest occasions they have ever enjoyed. And that, I think, is the measure of Bert.

Paul Kelly

Mr Chairman, ladies and gentlemen, distinguished guests, friends and family of Bert Kelly.

Bert and I weren't related. But I was a great admirer of Bert, and I learnt a number of lessons from him. To me Bert Kelly was a modern thinker and a old-fashioned politician. I think as a modern thinker he was vindicated and as an old-fashioned politician he inspired affection and appreciation. One is tempted to say there are not too many modern thinkers and very few old-fashioned politicians left these days.

There are three great qualities Bert Kelly had as far as I was concerned – clarity, courage and responsibility.

Clarity is an important quality for a politician. It is impossible for a politician to master all areas of policy and all areas of government. A politician must be selective. A politician must have judgement. Above all a politician must have clarity if he is to leave his mark. Bert Kelly had clarity. He was able to see beneath the surface and it is not always easy to see beneath the surface. I appreciate the need to expose all sorts of government rorts, whether travel allowances or overseas trips. But it is even more important to look beneath the surface at massive and hidden transfers of wealth and income. That is what Bert could do and that was the value of his clarity.

The other day I reread sections of his book *One More Nail*. It is interesting that the first point he makes in the Introduction is the fundamental point in the tariff debate: that tariffs don't save jobs. I think it is significant that this is what he said at the start, and it was the message all the way through. It was clarity about the fact that tariffs inhibit growth and lead to a transfer of resources to inefficient industries thereby hurt-

---

Paul Kelly is International Editor of The Australian.

ing the export sector.

The next great virtue of Bert's was courage. I value highly courage in a politician because I have spent a large part of the last 25 years dealing with politicians, having discussions with them about policy matters, being told repeatedly that they know that a particular policy is the right policy (and by that they mean they mean the right policy for the country), but they are not in a position to advocate that policy at the moment for good and sound political reasons.

I remember one of the comments John Hyde made to me about Bert many years ago. John said that when he was campaigning against protection, when he stood up and fought the cause in the Liberal Party room, that he was never alone. He always had people supporting him – admittedly a minority, just a small group. But the point about Bert was that he was alone. Bert did it by himself. This is a tremendous achievement in terms of courage. Not only did he do it by himself but he did it against enormous forces, and he did it for a very considerable period of time. He used all sorts of techniques I think, to sell his message and also to encourage himself during many times of depression. David Kemp has told the joke about the New Zealand race horse tariff. Bert was an old-fashioned politician who used parables to great effect. When we look at the enormous progress this country has made in terms of the tariff debate over the last couple of decades we should pay tribute to Bert. Bert was the longest crusader and for much of the time he was a solo crusader. A great tribute is warranted for his efforts.

The third value that I have identified is responsibility. This is a very complicated issue in politics. What is a proper sense of political responsibility? What is the obligation of the parliamentarian to his electorate, to his state and to his country? Bert believed firmly that ideas make and break history. Ideas also make or break countries and Bert took his stand on ideas. Bert believed that the idea that he was championing was the right idea and he decided to keep pursuing that idea in the interest of his electorate, his state and his country.

Those to me were the three great qualities – clarity, courage, responsibility.

It is a great shame Bert is not with us today because the caravan moves on. It is one of the eternal fascinations of politics that issues evolve and develop and, of course, the curve of progress is never perfectly even. You don't move uniformly in a particular direction. You get there with bumps and setbacks along the way. It is interesting to reflect upon where we are now as a country and the contemporary forces which are shaping the debate about protection. Let me stress that Bert's position was economically valid and the moral position that Bert took against tariffs was true. I think that moral position is enormously important. But there are, none the less, new political forces at work.

I would like to talk briefly about some of those forces because I think they are relevant for an audience such as this. I have two reactions to the current surge in protectionist sentiment on the part of the Labor Party and certain Liberal Premiers and backbenchers.

One is to wonder whether there is a form of collective amnesia at work, by which I mean a failure to remember the intellectual debates of the past in which Bert played such a role. Australia is a country not just with a long history of protection, but one which contributed so much internationally to understanding how protection works, to understanding who gains and who loses from protection, that it ill-behoves us as a nation to forget the intellectual progress that we have made. There is a risk that this may be happening. You see there are a lot of people involved in the debate today who have never heard of Bert Kelly or Alf Rattigan or the Industries Assistance Commission or probably of John McEwen. So an important lesson is that the intellectual debate must always be continued with vigour and vigilance, and Bert is an example of that.

But my second reaction is not to be surprised by some of the current fashion of protectionist sentiment. Let me identify some of the factors that drive it. The first is the high level of unemployment, about eight and a half per cent, but in reality much higher. High unemployment is always a tough political environment in which to make the argument for lower protection. We should bear in mind that the debate about the labour market and the debate about protection are always tied together. It is the people who oppose labour market reforms which we know will lower the level of unemployment who usually pretend that maintaining protection will save jobs. It is important that we bear in mind the connection between labour market reform and the high level of unemployment as this is tied inevitably to the debate about protection policy.

The next point that I would like to highlight is the cultural concern in the community that market solutions are ruthless in relation to human beings. Now this is where we can learn a lot from one of the points that Bert made about the morality of the low tariff position. At the moment in western democracies there is a powerful prejudice that a lot of economic reform proposals and market based solutions are against the interest of the individual and the interest of a sound and stable society. We need to be very careful about this notion as it is driven by some of the consequences of economic reform, in particular the significant increase in income and wealth inequalities which stem from some economic reform, as well as more lurid speculations that market orientated societies lack a moral basis. We can learn here from Bert when we read his book and look at some of the arguments that he mounted. He usually brought the argument back to a moral base. I think it is important that economic reformers today bring their arguments back to a moral base.

I think another relevant point to make is that there is in our communities a pervasive sense of job insecurity. It has been remarked upon by Alan Greenspan in analysing some of the reasons why the United States recovery has been so successful for so long. One of the points which Mr Greenspan has made is that it is the pervasive sense of job insecurity on the part of those people in jobs which has led to wage rates being lower then they otherwise would be, which in turn, has led to interest rates being lower then they otherwise would be. This has contributed to the length of the economic recovery. Now, if Mr Greenspan puts so much weight on this factor of job insecurity then I think we should recognise that this is an important motivational factor in our communities. It is a factor which is making people apprehensive and concerned about economic reform. It is a vital element we should bear in mind.

Finally, it seemed to me when I read the Productivity Commission report on the car industry that there is an intellectual debate being joined here. I refer in particular to the minority report from the industry representative Ian Webber. That minority report made a number of very strong points, which have a degree of support in the community. These points constitute an intellectual case against the low protection paradigm. I would like to refer to that minority opinion and to highlight its arguments.

First, it was argued that until Australia made more significant progress on domestic economic reform then it was inadvisable to continue protection cuts for the car industry when the present arrangements expire. In one sense this is an old argument. It overlooks the fact that protection cuts are in Australia's interests. However, I think it is a clever argument to be putting at this stage. When one looks at the commentary on the Howard government a lot of it is to the effect that the pace of domestic reform is too slow. If the pace of domestic reform is slower then it otherwise should be then this can be turned into an argument for a pause in protection levels for the car industry.

The next argument put in the minority report was that Australia should not proceed with unilateral action on tariffs, and that it was important instead for Australia to elicit binding commitments to lower protection from our trading partners. This is a far-reaching statement because it would represent a significant change in tariff policy. The way tariff policy has been conducted in recent times is that Australia has been prepared to make unilateral commitments in our own interests, which have later been folded into global arrangements. The argument that is being put in the minority report leaves hanging the assumption that somehow Australia has bargaining power to extract concessions on tariffs from our trading partners. It is a complete fantasy, of course. But this is a popular argument, namely that we shouldn't take unilateral action but wait and act when binding commitments are made by our trading partners, so action is on a reciprocal basis. It is a spurious proposition which has no validity in its own right and whose real purpose is to achieve a tariff pause.

The third point made is that regional pain outweighs the national gain in terms of more protection cuts for the car industry. This is a clever argument because you can identify where the pain is, whereas the gains are spread. It has currency today with non-Labor governments in power in Canberra and in most States.

The next argument was the assumption that regardless of the APEC deadlines it is virtually inevitable that there will be special arrangements made to exempt the motor vehicle industry from the APEC protection reduction timetables. The point to make about this is that if Australia argues this case then we are inviting the unravelling of the APEC timetables by encouraging all other APEC members to put forward their own special case and their own special exemption. It will backfire on us.

The fifth point was that because protection has been reduced so much, future gains from even lower protection are modest compared to earlier gains. Because the benefits are less we therefore have less to lose if we hold protection at present levels. I think again this is a clever argument because there is some truth in it. But it is designed to play upon another reality, and this is the political reality that the more you cut tariffs the harder it is to keep going.

I think, overall, these are important arguments. I believe that the community understands a lot of these arguments. They are being put with great frequency on talkback radio in Sydney and Melbourne and they have been taken up by a number of so called cultural icons in the media. We need to be particularly alert and alive to the growth of these ideas.

My final remark is that this is an intellectual debate. It is vital that the debate be conducted with considerable rigour and vigilance. I believe the protection issue today is largely over the rate at which Australia continues to cut protection. But this debate is important in terms of economic progress and in terms of the economic and political culture over the next five to ten years. It is related to the rate at which other economic reforms are made. Beyond that it is related to regional institutions such as APEC and, at the end of the day, the delivery of Australian foreign policy. I believe that in continuing the ongoing debate about protection we should bear in mind the methodology and virtues that Bert Kelly brought to it.